Snakes

NATURE'S PREDATORS

Kris Hirschmann

KIDHAVEN
PRESS™

THOMSON

™

GALE

San Diego • Detroit • New York • San Francisco • Cleveland
New Haven, Conn. • Waterville, Maine • London • Munich

© 2003 by KidHaven Press. KidHaven Press is an imprint of The Gale Group, Inc., a division of Thomson Learning, Inc.

KidHaven™ and Thomson Learning™ are trademarks used herein under license.

For more information, contact
KidHaven Press
27500 Drake Rd.
Farmington Hills, MI 48331-3535
Or you can visit our Internet site at http://www.gale.com

LIBRARY OF CONGRESS CATALOGING-IN-PUBLICATION DATA

Hirschmann, Kris, 1967–
  Snakes / by Kris Hirschmann.
    p. cm. — (Nature's predators)
  Includes bibliographical references (p.   ) and index.
    Summary: Describes the predatory nature of snakes, the various methods used to hunt and kill prey, the process used to eat and digest prey, and ultimately when hunter becomes hunted.
    ISBN 0-7377-1006-3 (hardback : alk. paper)
    1. Snakes—Juvenile literature. [1. Snakes.] I. Title. II. Series.
  QL666. O6 H64 2003
  597.96—dc21

  2001005691

Printed in the United States of America

Contents

Chapter 1

Born Hunters

There are around twenty-seven hundred different species (types) of snakes in the world. Each of these species has its own unique characteristics. For example, a snake may be tiny (the smallest snakes measure just four inches from nose to tail tip) or enormous (up to thirty-three feet long). Some species bear colorful markings, while others have dull, drab skins. Each species has its own special way of moving, resting, and eating. All of these differences make it possible to tell one type of snake from another.

When it comes to their basic purpose in life, however, all snakes are alike in one important way. They are all **carnivores**, which means that they survive by eating the flesh of other animals. And they are all skilled **predators** whose lifestyles and bodies are perfectly adapted to meet their food needs.

Snake Basics

Snakes are members of the reptile family, which also includes lizards, crocodilians, turtles, tortoises, and tuataras (iguana-like creatures). Snakes are the newest reptiles on earth. Fossil records show that the first snakes appeared about 130 million years ago, hundreds of millions of years after the earliest reptiles.

In this period of time snakes have become one of the world's most successful and widespread animal families. Today snakes live on every continent except Antarctica, and they can be found in almost every type of habitat. Land-dwelling snakes make their homes in hot deserts, on forest floors, in treetops, and in underground burrows. Freshwater snakes lurk in ponds, lakes, and streams throughout the world. There are even about fifty species of sea snakes that swim the Pacific and Indian Oceans.

Snakes eat a wide variety of animals, including insects, worms, frogs, lizards, fish, birds, mammals, and other snakes. They also eat the eggs of other animals. Some types of snakes are specialists that prey only on certain creatures, while others will eat anything they can catch.

A snake's size plays an important part in its diet. Small snakes eat small prey. A large snake can easily swallow dogs, cats, goats, and other medium-sized mammals. And the biggest snakes have been known to eat truly gigantic meals: A 30-foot rock

Snake Shapes and Sizes

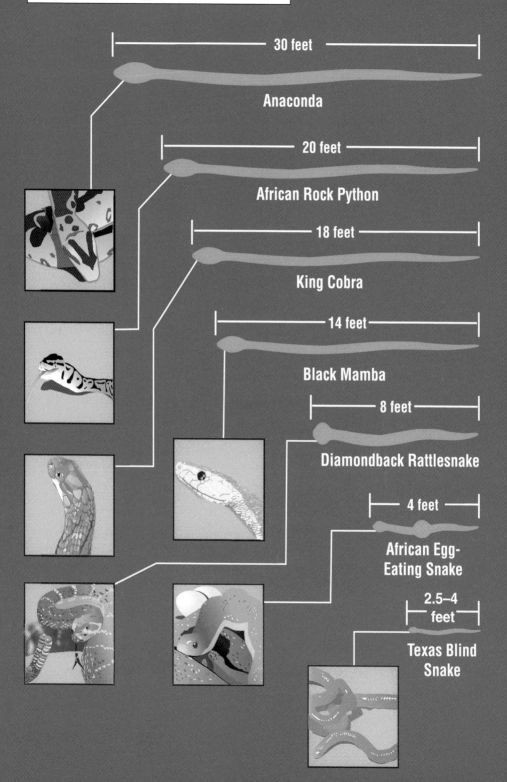

30 feet

Anaconda

20 feet

African Rock Python

18 feet

King Cobra

14 feet

Black Mamba

8 feet

Diamondback Rattlesnake

4 feet

African Egg-Eating Snake

2.5–4 feet

Texas Blind Snake

python was once seen gulping down a 130-pound impala!

A snake's size also determines the frequency with which it hunts and eats. Small, active snakes hunt almost continually and may eat several times a day. Large, sluggish snakes hunt only once in a while and may go weeks between meals.

Watchful Eyes

No matter what it eats, a snake has a number of built-in weapons that help it to hunt and catch prey. The first of these weapons is vision.

The importance of vision varies between species. Some snakes have excellent eyesight and depend on this sense while hunting. Other snakes have poor vision. They can see motion and shades of light, but not much more. And some underground snakes do not even have eyes. They are completely blind.

The position of the eyes also varies between species. Daytime hunters that rely on their eyesight usually have forward-pointing eyes. This arrangement helps a snake to judge distance accurately. Other types of snakes have eyes on the sides of their head. These snakes have a wider field of vision than forward-looking snakes but cannot judge distance as well. Although they may use their eyes to spot prey, sideways-looking snakes depend on other senses when they attack.

Different snakes have different types of pupils. Snakes that hunt during the day, called **diurnal**

With eyes on the sides of its head, a green tree python has a wider field of vision than forward-looking snakes.

snakes, have round pupils that can get very small to block bright light. Snakes that hunt at night, called **nocturnal** snakes, have slit pupils that can open especially wide to catch the faintest glimmer of moonlight.

Sense of Smell

Although vision is useful to a snake, it is not nearly as important as the sense of smell. All snakes have excellent smelling abilities, and these abilities come in handy when it is time to hunt.

Snakes have two ways of smelling. Like humans and many other animals, snakes have two nostrils through which they breathe air. As the snake breathes, sensory cells inside the nostrils detect airborne scent particles. The sensory cells send messages about the particles to the snake's brain, which then "decodes" the messages.

Snakes also use their tongues to help them smell. A snake sticks its forked tongue out of a notch in its upper lip, then flicks the tongue rapidly

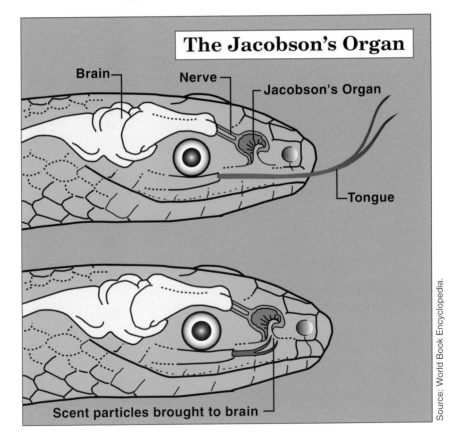

The Jacobson's Organ

Brain — Nerve — Jacobson's Organ

Tongue

Scent particles brought to brain —

Source: World Book Encyclopedia.

to collect scent particles from the air. When the snake pulls its tongue back in, the scent particles move through openings in the top of the mouth into a structure called **Jacobson's organ**. Like the sensory cells in the nose, Jacobson's organ then sends scent messages to the brain to be decoded.

Between the two tips of its forked tongue, a snake can detect tiny differences in scent. This ability allows snakes to track their prey. A hunting snake flicks its tongue over and over, gathering particles and judging where the prey scent is strongest. By changing its direction according to these scents, a snake soon finds its intended victim.

"Seeing" Heat

Some types of snakes, including boas, pythons, and pit vipers, have special features called **pit organs** that can detect the body heat of prey. Using these organs, a snake clearly "sees" its warm prey against leaves, the ground, or any other cool object.

Boas and pythons have many pit organs around the lips and snout. Pit vipers, including rattlesnakes, bushmasters, and the fer-de-lance, have just two deep pits, one on each side of the head between the eye and the nostril.

A snake's heat sense is especially useful for night hunting. Even when it is too dark to see, a snake with pit organs can easily find birds and other warm-blooded prey. Being able to sneak up on sleeping prey is a big advantage for a hungry snake, so many pit snakes feed mostly at night.

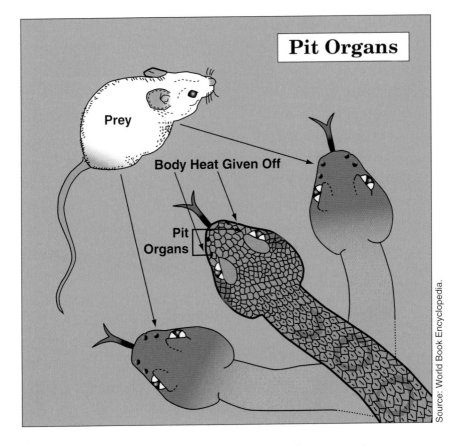

Source: World Book Encyclopedia.

Besides helping a snake to find prey, pit organs have another important function. They help a snake to direct its **strike**. Tiny differences in the heat detected by different pit organs tell a snake exactly where its prey is. The snake's strike will therefore be accurate—and deadly.

Mouth, Teeth, and Fangs

A snake uses its senses to find prey. To kill and eat, it uses another weapon: its mouth.

The mouth's first job is to catch and hold prey. Although a snake may coil its body around another animal, this technique does not provide a secure grip. A firm bite does a better job. So all snakes have mouths full of tiny, sharp, backward-curving teeth. The arrangement of the teeth makes it very hard for prey to break loose.

Many snakes also have pointed, hollow teeth called **fangs** that can inject **venom** into their prey. Some snakes have long, hinged fangs that retract into the roof of the mouth when not in use. Other snakes have smaller fangs that are fixed in place. But whatever their arrangement, all fangs work the same way. A snake sinks its fangs into a prey's flesh, then pumps venom into the body through the hollow tooth shafts. The venom disrupts the prey's bodily functions, paralyzing or killing the animal

Venom drips off a prairie rattlesnake's fang. When a snake injects venom into its prey it paralyzes or kills the animal.

so the snake can eat it without danger of being harmed.

A snake's mouth has one last amazing function. Flexible jaws allow a snake to stretch its mouth wider than its body. This ability lets a snake swallow prey that is bigger than the snake's own head.

Other Weapons

Snakes have many other weapons that help them to hunt. They may use their senses of hearing, touch, and even taste. Their slender bodies can slide into narrow openings, and their flexibility lets them enter awkward areas. A snake may be colored in a way that helps it to sneak up on its prey, or it may be able to move so silently that prey never hears it coming. All of these abilities combine with a snake's vision, sense of smell, and mouth to make this animal one of the world's most efficient predators.

Chapter 2

Hunting and Killing

In general, snakes prefer to catch their own meals. (The North American water moccasin, sometimes called the cottonmouth, is the only exception. It sometimes eats carrion.) To get live prey, snakes must chase and catch other animals. But compared to many of the animals on which they feed, snakes cannot travel very fast. They do not have any limbs to help them grab prey, and they often feed on creatures larger than themselves.

Despite these limitations, snakes have no trouble finding or subduing food. This is because snakes are skilled predators. They have many effective hunting and killing techniques that give them the advantage over their prey.

Active Hunters

Some snakes are active hunters. This means that they go looking for prey rather than waiting for

A large black rat snake chases a mouse. Sometimes snakes have to give chase to quick-moving prey.

prey to come to them. The "find-and-chase" strategy works very well for snakes that eat snails, slugs, and other slow-moving creatures. When one of these snakes finds prey, it simply moves its body into a convenient eating position and gobbles down its meal.

The chase is not as easy for snakes that eat lizards, rodents, and other quick-moving animals. But a few species of snakes enjoy great success with this technique. Whipsnakes and sand snakes sometimes flush prey animals out of their hiding places, then chase them for short distances. Some types of snakes follow mice and rats into their burrows, cornering them so they cannot run away. And some sea snakes poke their heads into the nooks and crannies between underwater rocks and coral, looking for tasty fish. When they find one, they use their bodies to block any exits, then deliver a killing bite to the trapped prey.

Ambush Hunters

Most snakes do not chase their prey. Instead, they hide and wait for prey to come to them. This ambush technique is safer and easier than active hunting, but it is less certain because there is no guarantee that prey animals will come along. To increase its chances of catching a meal, an ambush hunter usually settles in an area where prey is plentiful. The snake will feed until the prey population gets too low. Then it will move to a new, less hunted area.

To be successful, an ambush hunter must not be noticed by its prey. For this reason, many ambush hunters have special skin coloring that

A Gaboon viper eats a mouse. The snake's body pattern and colorization allows it to blend with the forest floor and ambush prey.

makes them hard to see. The Gaboon viper, for example, has a blotchy body pattern that breaks up the snake's outline against leaves or other textured backgrounds. The green tree python, whose body is a smooth emerald green, is tough to spot in its tree-top home. And the sidewinder rattlesnake's brown body perfectly matches its desert surroundings.

Not all ambush hunters have special coloring. Some just hide from their prey. The green anaconda, for example, submerges its huge body in the shallow water near the edges of ponds and streams. When prey comes to drink, the anaconda springs out of its hiding place and grabs its meal. Some fish-eating snakes do exactly the opposite: They look into the water from above, waiting for fish to swim past. When they spot a tasty creature, they dive into the water and seize their startled prey.

The Strike

Once a snake has found its prey, it catches it with a lightning-quick lunge called a strike. To prepare for the strike, a snake curves its body into a coil. It points its head toward the prey and tightens its muscles. When the prey is within reach, the snake uses its coiled body like a spring to shove its head forward. This movement is very fast—so fast, in fact, that it cannot be followed by the human eye.

The snake's mouth is closed at the beginning of the strike. While the head is traveling toward the prey, however, the mouth opens. If the snake has hinged fangs, it shifts them out of their pockets. By the time the snake's head reaches its target, the mouth is wide open and the teeth and fangs are pointing nearly straight at the prey.

The force of the strike drives these weapons into the prey's flesh, wounding the animal. The strike also stuns the prey, giving the snake a chance to clamp its jaws shut. The snake's backward-curving

---

With its mouth open wide, an eyelash viper strikes at a hummingbird.

teeth plunge deeper into the prey's body as the mouth closes. At the same time, the prey is dragged toward the hungry predator's throat.

After the Strike

If the prey is small enough, the snake may swallow it on the spot. Larger prey, however, are much too dangerous to be eaten alive. A kicking, scratching animal could badly hurt a snake, and so these animals must be killed before they can be eaten.

The killing process starts the moment a snake bites into its prey. Caught in the snake's mouth, the still-living prey struggles to escape. But its thrashing motions do it no good. The snake's teeth slice deeper and deeper into the prey's flesh with each kick and squirm.

Nonvenomous snakes rest quietly after the strike, letting the prey's own motions do all the damage. Before long the prey will die from its wounds, and the snake will be ready to eat its meal. More than 80 percent of snakes have no venom, so this passive killing method is very common in the snake world.

Venomous snakes that have short front fangs or fangs near the back of the mouth inject their venom in the moments following the strike. They do this by chewing on their prey. Once the venom is injected, the snake simply waits for it to take effect before starting the eating process. Cobras use this method. So do kraits, mambas, coral snakes, and sea snakes.

A lava lizard's sharp claws are no help in the paralyzing grasp of a dromicus snake.

Vipers and pit vipers have the easiest job of all. Their long, hinged fangs "stab" prey during the strike, injecting venom the moment they break the flesh. A snake of this type often releases its prey after the strike, letting it wander away to die from the effects of the venom. The snake then tracks and eats the fresh carcass. Rattlesnakes, which are among the snake family's most dangerous killers, are well known for this behavior.

Squeezed to Death

A few types of snakes, including pythons and boas, kill their prey by a process called **constriction**.

Like other snakes, a constrictor catches its prey by striking. But instead of waiting for the prey to die, the constrictor squeezes it to death. Biting firmly to keep its meal from escaping, the snake wraps its powerful body around the prey. Each time the prey breathes out, the snake tightens its coils just enough so the prey cannot breathe in again. The snake repeats this process until the prey suffocates.

Constrictor snakes are the giants of the reptile world. The green anaconda of South America, the African rock python, and the reticulated python of southeastern Asia may all grow to more than thirty feet in length. Snakes of this size are terrifying to

An anaconda squeezes the life out of a caiman.

people, who fear being eaten. But although a large constrictor *could* consume a human being, there is no proof that this has ever happened.

Skilled Predators

With their hunting and killing abilities, snakes have little trouble finding the food they need to survive. It is no wonder that most creatures, including many larger and faster animals, take pains to avoid these dangerous predators.

Chapter 3

Eating and Digesting

For most predators, eating is a simple process that involves tearing off and swallowing bite-sized chunks of flesh. For snakes, however, it is not so easy. Snakes have no tearing teeth, which means they must swallow their prey whole. Snakes also do not have arms or legs they could use to shove food into their mouths, and their weak tongues are no help during the swallowing process.

Given these facts, it seems incredible that snakes can gobble down even large prey. Thanks to their amazing mouths and bodies, however, snakes are able to eat and digest just about anything they can catch. A snake's unusual eating methods keep the snake well fed—and strong enough to kill over and over again.

Small animals are the easiest prey for a snake to handle. Animals smaller than the snake's mouth and throat can be easily gulped down. If an animal

A rough tree snake stalks a butterfly. Smaller snakes survive by eating easy meals like insects and worms.

is not dangerous to the snake, it may even be swallowed alive. Insects, worms, lizards, and smaller snakes therefore make easy meals, and hundreds of species of small- to medium-sized snakes survive by eating such prey.

Insects and other small animals, however, do not provide enough nourishment for a really big snake, which needs lots of food to fuel its large body. So large snakes like boas and pythons tend to hunt large prey. Big birds and medium-sized mammals make good meals, but they are harder to eat; they cannot be easily gobbled down. Snakes therefore use a different and more cautious technique when eating larger prey.

The first step is to make sure the prey is not dangerous. Mice and other small animals cannot do much harm, so a snake that catches one of these creatures may begin the swallowing process immediately after the strike. But bigger animals might kick and scratch, hurting the snake. Therefore, a snake that catches a larger animal will wait until the prey is dead before beginning to eat. Venomous snakes may start the process a little earlier if they are sure that their prey is paralyzed.

When a snake's prey can no longer move, the snake releases its biting grip. It moves around the prey, flicking its forked tongue to sniff out the carcass's head. Once the head is found, the snake shifts its body and takes the head into its mouth. By swallowing the prey head first, the snake ensures that the legs, wings, tail, and other body parts will slide easily down its throat.

Swallowing

The snake bites hard into the head, anchoring its sharp teeth in the prey's flesh. The snake then begins to produce huge amounts of saliva. The saliva has two purposes. It starts the digestion process, and it also lubricates the snake's mouth and throat so the prey can slide in as easily as possible.

When everything is good and slippery, the snake starts to move its jaws. The right and left sides of a snake's jaws can move independently,

A corn snake swallows a rat headfirst so its legs and tail will slide easily down the snake's throat.

and the snake uses this ability to force prey into its throat. The snake first pulls back with one side of its mouth. When the snake has pulled as far as it can, it bites and pulls with the other side of its mouth. At the same time, it releases the first side and moves it back into biting position. The snake repeats this movement over and over, alternating sides each time. With each pull, the prey is yanked a little farther into the snake's gullet until it finally disappears.

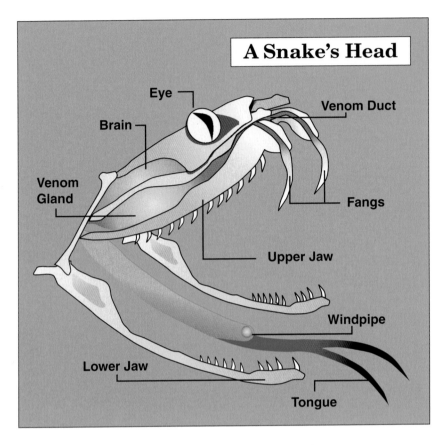

A Snake's Head

Eye

Venom Duct

Brain

Venom
Gland

Fangs

Upper Jaw

Windpipe

Lower Jaw

Tongue

A snake can even use this technique to eat animals bigger than its own head. The snake's many jaw bones simply shift apart as the snake swallows, temporarily increasing the size of the snake's head and mouth. The flexible skin of the throat also gets larger, stretching as the meal enters.

It typically takes a snake two to five minutes to swallow a meal. But the time varies with the size of the prey. A garter snake might gobble down a small slug in a few seconds, while a huge python might take several hours to swallow a goat or another large animal.

After the Meal

Once the prey has been swallowed, the snake makes a series of yawning motions to put its jaws back into place. The snake also twists its body repeatedly to force its meal into the stomach. If the prey is large, the snake's elastic skin stretches as the animal passes deeper into the body. From the outside, the prey can easily be seen as a bulge in the snake's midsection.

A snake that has eaten a large animal will be sluggish until it digests its meal. This postmeal period can be dangerous for snakes, which depend on their speed and agility to defend themselves. Many snakes therefore speed up the digestion process by basking in the sun. The sun warms the snake and causes all of its bodily functions, including digestion, to function more quickly. Before long the prey has been absorbed and the snake is ready to hunt again.

The bigger the meal, the longer it takes to digest. So snakes avoid unusually large meals if possible. But a hungry snake may eat a wild pig, a deer, or another especially large animal every now and then. After the meal, the snake's belly is so swollen that the snake has trouble moving. It may take days for the snake to dissolve its meal down to a manageable size, and the snake may not eat again for months.

Some Unusual Eaters

Although most snakes use similar eating techniques, a few snakes have some unusual tricks and habits.

African egg-eating snakes feed on bird eggs. These snakes can swallow eggs two to three times larger than their own heads. An egg-eating snake pushes its open mouth against an egg, slowly shoving the egg into its body. When the egg enters the throat, it is cracked open by sharp spines. The runny insides of the egg trickle down the snake's throat, and the snake spits out the empty shell.

Some snail-eating snakes have hook-shaped jaws that can scoop snails out of their shells. Other snail eaters bite into the flesh of their prey, then jam the snail's shell between two stationary objects and twist until the body pops out.

An African egg-eating snake prepares to crush a large bird egg.

A ringed snail-eating snake hovers above a snail,
preparing to strike.

Some insect eaters also have an unusual way of
eating. These snakes puncture their prey's hard ex-
oskeleton (outer shell), then suck out the innards.
No matter what they eat or how they eat it, all
snakes have one thing in common. They are born
killers that must eat to survive—and nature has
given them all the tools they need to fulfill this purpose.

Chapter 4

Snakes as Prey

Although snakes are skilled hunters, they are not the only predators out looking for food. Many hungry animals roam the same areas where snakes are found—and many of these animals are bigger and stronger than snakes. If a snake encounters one of these predators, it is likely to find itself on the menu.

Snake Predators

Snakes have a wide variety of enemies. Nearly all predatory birds and mammals will eat snakes if they get the chance. Lizards will prey on snakes, and so will alligators, crocodiles, frogs, toads, and turtles. Sea snakes make a tasty meal for large fish. Even spiders, scorpions, and fire ants will attack and eat snakes if the opportunity arises.

Snakes are not even safe from their own kind. Large snakes often feed on small snakes. In fact, a few types of snakes, including pipe snakes and coral snakes, eat almost nothing *but* other snakes. And the king cobra, a sixteen-foot predator found in Asia, is a true snake specialist. It will not touch any other kind of food.

Some animals find snake meat so tasty that they have become snake-killing experts. The African secretary bird, which uses its clawed feet to stamp snakes to death, is one such predator. The roadrunner, a bird that lives in southwestern America, is another. And the Indian gray mongoose

A Savannah monitor bites into a spitting cobra. Large lizards are one of the many predatory enemies of snakes.

A cat-eyed snake does not stand a chance against the snake-eating coral snake.

is an especially nimble snake killer. This small mammal darts at a snake, provoking it to strike over and over again. When the snake is exhausted, the mongoose zips in and kills it with a hard bite to the head.

Staying Out of Sight

A snake's best defense against predators is staying out of sight. Hiding is the easiest way to do this, so many snakes spend a lot of time resting in underground burrows, in dense growth, under dead leaves, or in other hidden spots.

A snake's coloring can also keep it from being noticed. The same skin patterns and camouflage that help a snake to sneak up on its prey also hide the snake from larger animals that may be looking for a meal.

Some snakes' bodies bear bright rings and stripes that make the snake difficult to spot against multicolored backgrounds. Not only do these markings keep the snake hidden, they also protect the snake if it must flee from a predator. The contrasting colors break up the snake's body outline as it moves, confusing the predator and giving the snake a chance to escape.

Flashy Markings

Although most types of snakes try to avoid being noticed, some use exactly the opposite technique. Instead of hiding or camouflaging themselves, these snakes bear bright, colorful markings that make them stand out from their surroundings. This is called **warning coloration**, and it usually means that a snake is either venomous or bad-tasting. Predators quickly learn to stay away from these colorful animals.

The venomous coral snake uses this method to protect itself. The coral snake's body bears brilliant red, yellow, and black bands. These colors scream "Danger!" to a predator, with the result that coral snakes are seldom bothered.

Some nonvenomous snakes take advantage of this situation by **mimicking** the coral snake's colors. Their markings do not exactly match the coral snake's, but the imitation is good enough to confuse a hungry bird or mammal. Most predators will play it safe, avoiding anything that looks like a coral snake—just in case.

Bluffing

A snake that is approached by a predator will retreat if possible. But if the snake cannot escape, it may try to scare the predator away by making itself seem more dangerous than it really is. This behavior is called bluffing, and most snakes do it when cornered.

Some snakes bluff by making their bodies bigger than normal. Cobras do this by opening flaps of skin around their head and neck, forming a broad hood. The boomslang snake inflates its throat, and the puff adder inflates its entire body.

Other snakes try to scare predators away by flashing bright colors or markings. Cottonmouth

Some nonvenomous snakes mimic coral snake patterns to confuse predators.

An eastern hognose snake plays dead to avoid being eaten by a predator.

snakes use this technique when threatened, opening their mouths to display the cottony-white tissue inside. Pipe snakes and ringneck snakes have colorful tails that they raise when attacked. And certain cobras have dark eye spots on their hoods. By displaying its colors, a snake may confuse a predator just long enough to escape.

A few snakes have even stranger tricks. Some play dead if a predator comes too close. Others release bad-smelling substances from their bodies. Some snakes can even bleed at will!

Warning

If bluffing does not scare a predator away, a snake goes into warning mode. It shifts its body into a defensive position, pulling all its muscles tight and pointing its head at the approaching animal. This

The large rattle of a black-tailed rattlesnake warns animals that they are too close.

posture tells the predator that the snake is getting ready to defend itself. If the predator comes any closer, the snake will strike.

Many snakes also make loud warning noises if another animal gets too close. The rattlesnake is famous for this behavior. This snake's tail ends in a series of loose, interlocking scales that bump loudly against each other when the tail tip is shaken. This rattling sound is the snake's way of telling other animals to back off—or suffer the consequences.

The rattlesnake is not the only noisemaker in the snake family. Other snakes make a variety of noises to warn predators away. Many snakes hiss by forcing air through narrow openings inside their mouths. Some snakes can rub their scales together to make threatening noises. And a few snakes even mimic the rattlesnake's rattle by rustling dry leaves with their tail tips.

Unfortunately for the snake, warning behaviors do not always stop a predator. If the predator ignores the warnings and continues to approach, the snake will strike—but the snake's best efforts may not be good enough. When a large and hungry predator attacks, a snake is likely to end up as a meal.

The Human Threat

Of all predators, humans pose the biggest threat to snakes. People kill enormous numbers of these animals each year.

Some snake killings are accidental. Commercial fishing activities, for example, kill hundreds of thousands of sea snakes each season. Also, human development and logging activities are destroying many snakes' habitats. With nowhere to go, the snakes that once lived in these areas are slowly dying off.

Many snakes are also killed deliberately for their commercial uses. The snake's scaly skin is made into handbags, boots, belts, and other products. Snake flesh is used to make some medicines,

A Vietnamese market displays snake meat for sale.

and it may also be eaten as food. Some countries regulate the production and sale of snake products, but many do not.

Conservationists who are working to protect snakes feel that education will help keep snake populations from dying out. Right now, many people are scared of snakes and have no interest in protecting them. But snakes are an essential part of the world food chain. When snakes eat other animals, they help to keep those populations under control. And when snakes themselves are eaten, they nourish other animals. If people can understand the snake's important role, their attitudes may change. Perhaps they will come to appreciate the power and beauty of the snake—one of nature's most magnificent predators.

Glossary

carnivore: Any animal that eats the flesh of other animals.

constriction: A killing method that involves squeezing with the coils.

diurnal: Active in the daytime.

fang: A hollow, pointed tooth that delivers venom.

Jacobson's organ: An organ of smell located above the roof of a snake's mouth.

mimic: An animal that copies the look or behavior of another animal.

nocturnal: Active at night.

pit organ: A snake's heat-sensing organ.

predator: Any animal that hunts other animals to survive.

strike: A quick forward lunge used to bite or catch other animals.

venom: A poisonous fluid that can be injected into other animals.

warning coloration: The bright colors or markings of bad-tasting or venomous snakes.

For Further Exploration

Books

Kelly Barth, *Snakes: Endangered Animals & Habitats.* San Diego: Lucent Books, 2001. Contains good information about endangered snake species.

Jennifer Owings Dewey, *Rattlesnake Dance: True Tales, Mysteries, and Rattlesnake Ceremonies.* Honesdale, PA: Boyds Mills Press, 1997. The author of this book describes three personal encounters she has had with rattlesnakes. The book also includes a wealth of snake fact and lore.

Sarah Lovett, *Extremely Weird Snakes.* Santa Fe, NM: John Muir, 1993. This book profiles the world's strangest snakes. It includes color photographs and illustrations.

David Manning, *Keeping Snakes.* Hauppage, NY: Barron's Educational Series, 2001. This book is a kids' guide to snake-keeping. It includes practical information on snake housing, feeding, anatomy, and life cycles.

Sy Montgomery, *The Snake Scientist*. Boston: Houghton Mifflin, 1999. Describes the work of scientists in Manitoba, Canada's Narcisse Wildlife Management Area, the site of the world's greatest concentration of snakes.

Websites

Awesome Snakes (www.everwonder.com). This fun site features snake games, videos, quizzes, and pictures.

Slither (www.slither.co.uk). Complete information on snake care and handling.

World of Reptiles (www.thesnake.org). This site has a lot of good information about snakes and other reptiles. It also has free wallpaper images to download and snake greeting cards to e-mail.

Index

Picture Credits

About the Author

Kris Hirschmann has written more than sixty books for children, mostly on science and nature topics. She is the president of The Wordshop, a business that provides a wide variety of writing and editorial services and she holds a bachelor's degree in psychology from Dartmouth College in Hanover, New Hampshire.

Hirschmann lives just outside of Orlando, Florida, with her husband, Michael.